Date: 8/2/12

CONTENTS

To Shoot or Not to Shoot

On the afternoon of February 19, 2009, Police **Sergeant** Greg Martin was in his car waiting at a traffic light in Ocala, Florida. Even though he was off duty, he listened carefully to a call coming in on his **two-way radio**. The **dispatcher** said that a robbery was in progress at a drugstore. Sergeant Martin realized that the store was across the street from where he was stopped. He quickly drove into the parking lot.

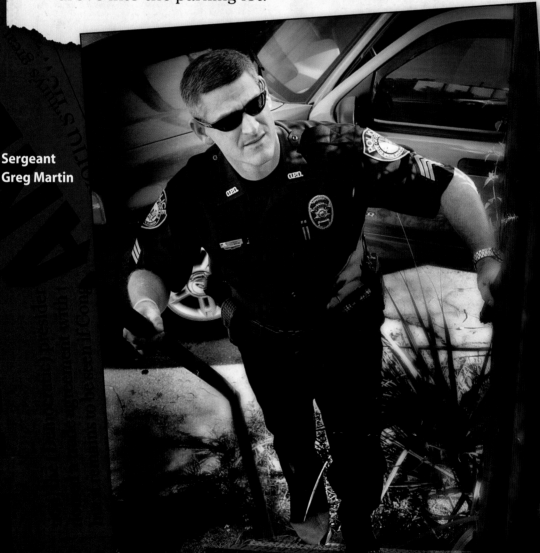

Sergeant
Greg Martin

Meanwhile, inside the drugstore, a masked man held the store's employees at gunpoint. He threatened to shoot them if they did not follow his orders. Suddenly, one of the employees grabbed the robber and pulled off his mask. **Panicked**, the robber ran out into the parking lot, unaware that Sergeant Martin was waiting with his gun drawn. The police officer had to quickly make an important decision— to shoot or not to shoot!

Police officers generally have the right to **enforce** the law at any time, even when they are not officially on duty. However, they must **identify** themselves as police officers before taking action.

The Right Choice

Sergeant Martin didn't want to shoot. He was worried that **innocent** people in the parking lot might get hurt in a shoot-out. So, with his gun aimed at the robber, he shouted, "Police! Drop your weapon!" The robber, however, didn't listen. He turned and started to run. Sergeant Martin ran after him and yelled, "Drop your weapon, or I'll shoot!"

In certain situations, police officers have to chase after the people they are trying to arrest.

In most cities, police officers are allowed to shoot at a suspect only if they have good reason to believe that they or other people are in danger of death or serious injury.

This time the robber dropped his gun, but he kept on running. Sergeant Martin continued chasing the robber. Finally, he was able to catch up with the man, wrestle him to the ground, and handcuff him. As a police officer, Sergeant Martin risks his life every day to stop dangerous criminals and save innocent people. For him, this arrest was just another day at the office.

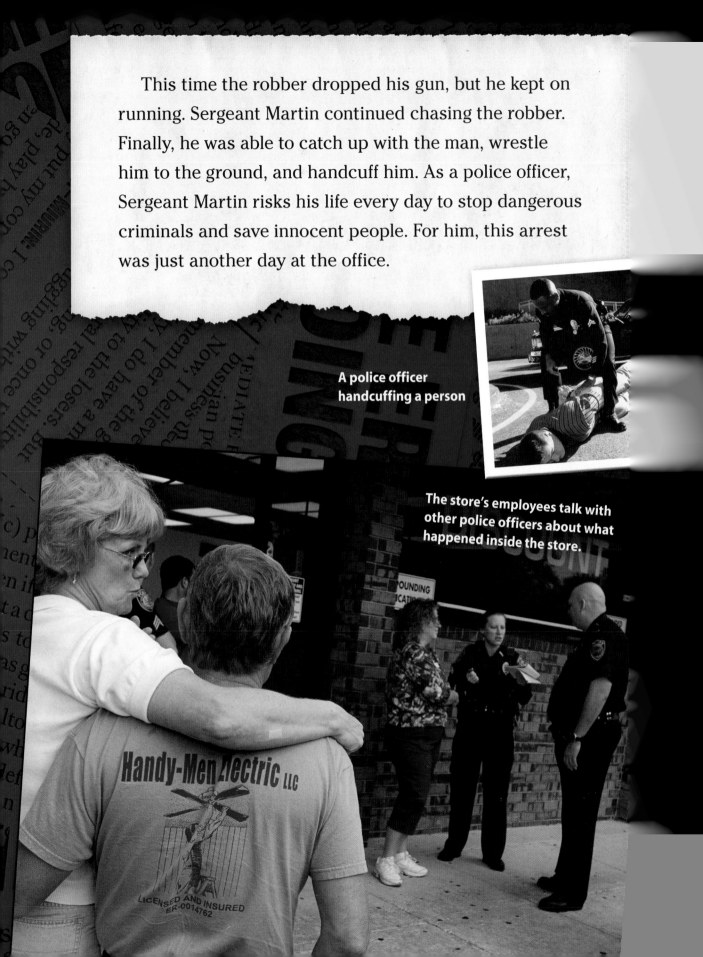

A police officer handcuffing a person

The store's employees talk with other police officers about what happened inside the store.

First on the Scene

Police officers such as Greg Martin have a very important job—to prevent crime and protect people and their property. Police officers serve their communities in different ways. They may **patrol** neighborhoods to stop crimes or direct traffic to keep the streets safe. They are also often the first people to show up when there is an accident, a fire, a **natural disaster**, or even a **terrorist** attack. All police officers are trained to know what to do when they arrive at any location in which people are in danger.

Police officers put up tape that says "POLICE LINE—DO NOT CROSS." This is to keep people out of dangerous areas.

Police officers help people stay safe by keeping them away from an accident or a disaster area.

At a disaster scene, the first thing police officers do is help people in the area get to a safe place. They also clear the area of cars and **onlookers**, so that firefighters and **paramedics** can easily reach the scene. Then, while waiting for the paramedics to arrive, they figure out which people need immediate medical care and give them **first aid**.

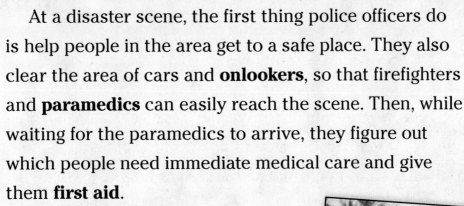

Police officers are trained to administer first aid until paramedics arrive.

Police officers are trained

It Takes Training

Knowing what to do when people are in danger takes special training. Though they may vary from police department to police department, the general requirements to begin police officer training are: be a U.S. citizen, be at least 18 years old, and be a high school graduate. Once these requirements are met, candidates need to pass physical fitness tests as well as tests that show they're **mentally** strong before being accepted into the **police academy**. Once training begins, students spend four to six months in classes learning **self-defense** skills, basic first aid, and how to use **firearms**.

This police a

While at the academy, students can specialize in different areas of police work. For example, some students want to learn more about emergency work and take advanced training in first-aid procedures. These students are also taught how to use emergency equipment, such as a **defibrillator**. Other students are interested in explosives and train for the **bomb squad**. They learn how to **deactivate** bombs or safely move them to an area where they can't damage buildings or hurt people if they explode. Though specialized training begins at the academy, it continues while an officer is on the job.

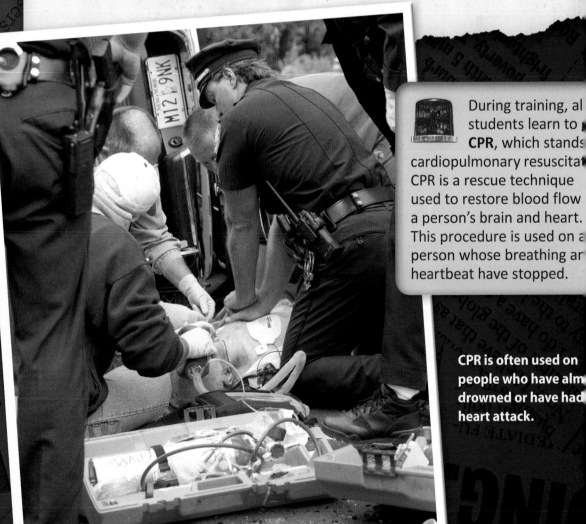

During training, al students learn to CPR, which stands cardiopulmonary resuscita CPR is a rescue technique used to restore blood flow a person's brain and heart. This procedure is used on a person whose breathing ar heartbeat have stopped.

CPR is often used on people who have alm drowned or have had heart attack.

Getting There

While at the police academy, students learn how to drive a police car during a special class called Emergency Vehicle Operator Course (EVOC). In EVOC, students are taught how to drive safely, even through heavy traffic, as they race to reach an emergency or chase a criminal.

All drivers learn that they should move to the right side of the road and, if possible, stop when they see flashing lights or hear a siren from a police car. This makes it easier for the police car to get through traffic quickly.

Students also learn that police vehicles are very different from regular cars. They have powerful engines that allow the cars to reach very high speeds. The cars have sirens and flashing lights to warn people to get out of the way, and loudspeakers so that officers inside the cars can broadcast information and warning messages to the public. Each police car also has special equipment such as a computer and a two-way radio, which an officer uses to get information and, when necessary, ask for **backup**.

A police officer can type the license plate number of a passing car into his or her computer. Within seconds, information about the car and the owner will come up on the screen.

 Police officers also use boats and helicopters to reach emergencies. For example, police officers in Chatham, Georgia, used a helicopter to find and rescue a grandmother and her grandchildren **stranded** in a small boat in a swamp.

A police helicopter making a water rescue

Teamwork Works!

On TV shows, police officers are often shown driving in a police car with a partner. However, police officers don't always work in pairs. Sometimes they patrol on their own.

A police officer patrolling a neighborhood

Whether they are working with a partner or not, police officers are part of a larger team. One of the key people on the team is the operator at a **communications center**. This person answers emergency calls to 911 and types up each caller's information—including the kind of emergency and the caller's name and address. Then the operator sends this information to a police dispatcher.

The dispatcher reads the information over a two-way radio that police officers in the area of the emergency can hear in their cars. Police vehicles that are closest to the emergency race to the scene as quickly as possible. Once there, if the situation is too dangerous or difficult for the officers to handle alone, they can radio the dispatcher to request backup.

It is important for an operator taking 911 calls to get as much information from the caller as possible, especially the exact location of the emergency.

Police officers and paramedics work together to get a wounded person to the hospital.

Often police officers, firefighters, and paramedics all work together as a team at the scene of a disaster.

First to Arrive

Police officers are often the first to show up at the scene of an accident. For example, Officer Stephen Blais of the West Warwick Police Department in Rhode Island was the first to arrive when an eight-year-old boy fell through the ice on Remington Pond. Fortunately, someone had been watching the pond from a nearby apartment building and called 911. The local fire department responded to the call with three fire engines and two rescue trucks.

It's very dangerous to play on a frozen lake. A person can easily fall through thin ice and get hurt or even drown.

To save the boy, Officer Blais went out onto the ice, still wearing his bulletproof vest and gun. He didn't want to waste the seconds it would take to remove the 20 pounds (9 kg) of equipment. Unfortunately, he fell through the ice while trying to rescue the boy. By the time the other responders arrived, Officer Blais was chest deep in the icy water, struggling to get the boy out. In the end, it was **Lieutenant** Paul McAllister, from the West Warwick Fire Department, who pulled the boy out of the freezing water.

Officer Blais (second from left) and Lieutenant McAllister (right) being honored for their heroic work

 After the boy was rescued, he was taken to Hasbro Children's Hospital in Providence, Rhode Island. He was cold and wet, but not seriously hurt.

Hasbro Children's Hospital

Tornado in Baltimore

Often, police officers are asked to help people after natural disasters such as tornadoes occur. For example, when a deadly tornado hit Baltimore, Maryland, in November 2010, many people's apartments were severely damaged. Calls to 911 began pouring in at around 2:00 A.M. Brave first responders raced to the scene and entered buildings that had been partially destroyed by the tornado. They tried to rescue people who were trapped and calling out for help.

A medium-strength tornado can overturn automobiles, rip off the roofs of houses, and uproot trees.

 Often police officers work with members of communities to help them prepare for natural disasters. For example, police departments may offer classes in basic first-aid techniques.

One of these heroes was Police Sergeant Michael Nichol. He rescued a woman buried by **debris** in her apartment. He told reporters, "A large piece of concrete was covering her. She couldn't move. She wasn't making any sounds either." Even though there was debris everywhere, the police officer was able to clear it away and pull the woman to safety.

More than 350 apartments were evacuated after the Baltimore tornado. Fortunately, no one died.

Bomb in Times Square

In addition to helping people during natural disasters, police officers are also ready to protect the public during acts of terrorism. On May 1, 2010, in New York City's Times Square, a man selling T-shirts on the sidewalk told Officer Wayne Rhatigan that he saw smoke coming from an **SUV**. After investigating the vehicle, Officer Rhatigan and two other officers called for backup and immediately directed hundreds of people away from the scene. They also put up **barriers** to keep the area clear. Within minutes, firefighters and the police department's bomb squad arrived. When the bomb squad broke a window of the SUV, they found that the car was packed with **explosive materials**.

On May 1, 2010, police officers evacuated New York City's Times Square, one of the most crowded places in the world.

It was later learned, from video cameras in the area, that a man had tried to light the explosives but they had failed to explode. Fortunately, they were deactivated before anyone was hurt or killed. Mayor Michael Bloomberg of New York City told reporters, "Thanks to alert New Yorkers and professional police officers, we avoided what could have been a very deadly event."

Bomb squads often us[e] robots with video cam[eras] to investigate bomb s[cenes.] Some robots also have special water pistols that can break bo[mbs] apart. Sending a robot instead [of a] person into a place where a bo[mb] may explode can save lives.

The New York City Police Department's bomb squad

A robot similar to this one was used to investigate the SUV in Times Square.

A Hero of 9/11

Heroic police officers also saved lives during the most horrible terrorist assault in U.S. history—the 2001 attack on New York City's World Trade Center. One of those heroes was Officer Moira Smith.

On September 11, 2001, terrorists flew two airplanes into the World Trade Center's twin towers.

Officer Smith was born and raised in Brooklyn, New York. She joined the New York City Police Department (NYPD) in 1988. Just three years later, in August 1991, five people were killed and more than 130 hurt in a subway crash in Union Square Station, one of New York City's busiest subway stations. Officer Smith was at the disaster scene, pulling out hurt and wounded people. She received the police department's Distinguished Duty Medal for saving dozens of lives that day.

Ten years later, on September 11, 2001, Officer Smith was among the first to report that a plane had crashed into the twin towers at the World Trade Center. She and her partner, Robert Fazio, rushed to the scene and began helping to evacuate the South Tower.

The crash in Un Square station was the secon subway disaste York City histo

When Officer Smith joined the NYPD, sh was a member of th transit bureau. The transit po are specially trained to handl crimes, accidents, and disast that occur on New York's sub trains or in the subway statio

She Gave Her Life

Inside the South Tower, Officer Smith calmly guided people down the stairs toward the exit. She looked people in the eye to make sure they were listening to her as she instructed them not to glance out the windows. She knew that if they saw the destruction outside they would panic. If that happened, people could endanger themselves or others. Officer Smith stayed calm, reassuring people that she would help them stay safe.

Officer Moira Smith is shown here helping a man get to safety minutes before the South Tower collapsed.

The people Officer Smith helped felt confident that she was in control of the situation, and followed her instructions. Many got out of the building safely. Sadly, Officer Smith never made it out herself. She was last heard from between the third and fourth floors, shortly before the tower collapsed. Her husband, Police Officer Jimmy Smith, told reporters, "She never got scared, never."

Twenty-three officers from the New York City Police Department died on September 11, 2001. Officer Moira Smith was the only woman among them.

Two police officers help a woman to safety after the attack on the twin towers.

Is This the Job for You?

Being a police officer is not easy. Anyone considering this as a career should think about the dangers that come with the job. Police officers can be injured or even killed in the line of duty. Even when they are off duty, they can be called in for an emergency. As a result, they are on call 24 hours a day, 7 days a week.

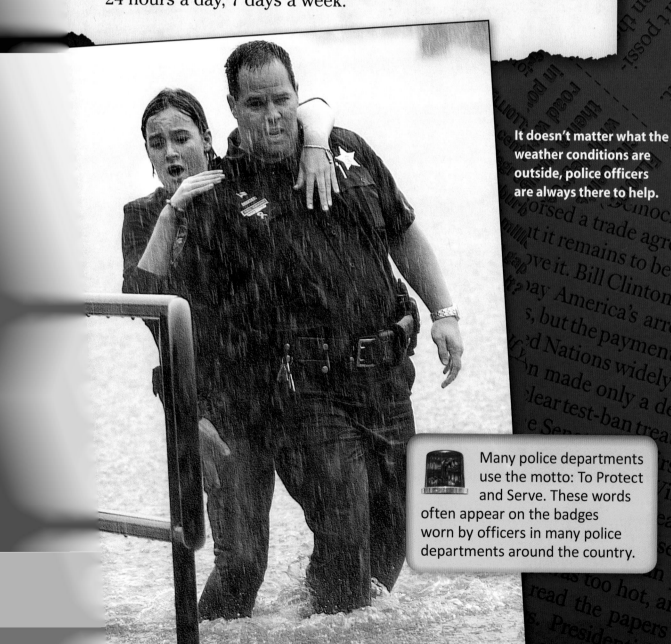

It doesn't matter what the weather conditions are outside, police officers are always there to help.

Many police departments use the motto: To Protect and Serve. These words often appear on the badges worn by officers in many police departments around the country.

Still, many police officers are so **dedicated** to helping others that they think they have the best job in the world. They feel pride when they save a life, and satisfaction when those they help express their thanks. It is this sense of pride and satisfaction that makes the officers feel that, although their job is filled with danger, they would not be happy with any other job in the world.

Police Officers' Gear

Police officers use gear that helps them catch criminals and protect themselves and others in dangerous situations. Here is some of their gear.

A *streamlight* is a powerful flashlight that lets a police officer see people and objects at night or in a dark building.

A *bulletproof vest* is made of a material that is light enough for an officer to wear all the time yet strong enough to stop a speeding bullet from wounding the wearer.

A *baton* is a stick or club that a police officer may use in a situation that does not call for shooting, but that requires more force than just the officer's bare hands. It can also be used to break down doors and break through windows to help trapped victims.

A police officer uses *handcuffs* when he or she arrests someone. The handcuffs prevent the person from fighting back or trying to hurt the officer.

A *handgun* is a small gun that can shoot accurately over a long distance. The bullets it shoots can badly wound or kill a person. A police officer uses a handgun only to stop a criminal from seriously hurting another person. A police officer keeps his or her gun in a *holster*.

Police officers also use gear that helps victims of crimes, accidents, or disasters. Here is some of the gear they use to help victims.

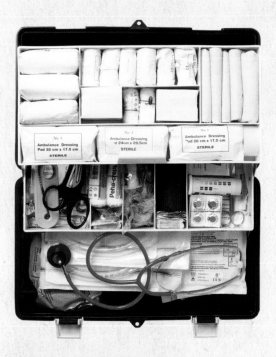

One of the most important pieces of equipment in a police officer's car is a *first-aid kit*. It contains many items, including bandages, tape, creams to soothe burns and wounds, a **tourniquet** to stop bleeding, and **sterile** gloves.

If a victim's heart has stopped, a *defibrillator* can start it beating again by giving the person electric shocks.

The *"jaws of life"* is a large tool that works like a giant can opener to cut off the roof or doors of a badly damaged vehicle. Police officers use it to help people who have been trapped in their cars after an auto accident.

Glossary

backup (BAK-up) support or help

barriers (BA-ree-urz) things that block the way

bomb squad (BOM SKWAHD) a team of police officers that respond to bomb threats

communications center (kuh-*myoo*-nuh-KAY-shunz SEN-tur) a place where people receive and send messages

CPR (see-pee-AR) the letters stand for cardiopulmonary resuscitation; a type of rescue where a person blows air into the mouth and then presses down on the chest of someone whose heart has stopped

deactivate (dee-AK-tuh-vayt) to make inactive

debris (duh-BREE) the scattered pieces of buildings or other objects that have been destroyed or damaged

dedicated (DED-uh-*kate*-id) devoted, loyal

defibrillator (dee-FIB-ruh-*lay*-tur) a machine that uses electric shock to restart patients' hearts

dispatcher (diss-PACH-ur) an operator who sends out people, usually in vehicles, to assist others

enforce (en-FORSS) to make sure that a law is obeyed

explosive materials (ek-SPLOH-siv muh-TIHR-ee-uhlz) substances that can blow up

firearms (FIRE-armz) weapons that shoot bullets

first aid (FURST AYD) care given to an injured or sick person in an emergency before he or she is treated by a doctor

identify (eye-DEN-tuh-fye) to tell who someone is

innocent (IN-uh-suhnt) not guilty

lieutenant (loo-TEN-uhnt) a fire or police department officer ranking below a captain

mentally (MEN-tuhl-ee) having to do with the mind

natural disaster (NACH-ur-uhl duh-ZASS-tur) an event caused by weather or nature that results in great damage or loss

onlookers (ON-luk-urz) people who watch an event taking place

panicked (PAN-ikt) terrified; filled with fear

paramedics (*pa*-ruh-MED-iks) people who are trained to respond to medical emergencies and take care of the injured until they arrive at the hospital

patrol (puh-TROHL) to walk or drive around an area to protect it, keep watch on people, and keep an eye out for trouble

police academy (puh-LEESS uh-KAD-uh-mee) a school that trains students to become police officers

self-defense (SELF-di-FENSS) the act of protecting oneself against attacks or threats

sergeant (SAR-juhnt) a police officer whose rank is above that of an ordinary officer

sterile (STER-uhl) completely clean; free from germs

stranded (STRAND-id) left somewhere without any way to get back home or to safety

SUV (*ess*-yoo-VEE) a sport-utility vehicle; a large car or small truck that can carry a lot of equipment

terrorist (TER-ur-ist) a person who uses violence and terror to get what he or she wants

tourniquet (TUR-nuh-ket) a bandage or piece of cloth twisted tightly around a part of a person's body to stop a wound from bleeding

two-way radio (TOO-way RAY-dee-oh) a radio that can both send and receive messages

Bibliography

Baker, Barry M. *Becoming a Police Officer.* New York: iUniverse (2006).

Hart, Alison. *Rescue: A Police Story.* New York: Random House (2002).

Sutton, Randy. *True Blue: Police Stories by Those Who Have Lived Them.* New York: St. Martin's Press (2005).

Whitlock, Charles R. *Police Heroes: True Stories of Courage about America's Brave Men, Women, and K-9 Officers.* New York: Thomas Dunne Books (2002).

Read More

Ethan, Eric. *Police Cars.* Milwaukee, WI: Gareth Stevens Publishing (2002).

Graham, Ian. *Emergency Vehicles.* Mankato, MN: Smart Apple Media (2009).

Johnston, Marianne. *Let's Visit the Police Station.* New York: PowerKids Press (2000).

Learn More Online

To learn more about police officers, visit
www.bearportpublishing.com/TheWorkofHeroes

Index

About the Author

Nancy White has written many nonfiction books for children. She lives just north of New York City, in the Hudson River Valley.